EMBRACED BY DIVINE LOVE

EMBRACED BY DIVINE LOVE

Contemplations to Transform Your Life

Dr. Joan Weathersbee Ellason

EMBRACED BY DIVINE LOVE

Contemplations to Transform Your Life

Dr. Joan Weathersbee Ellason

Copyright © 2025 Oasis Workshops with Dr. Joan Weathersbee Ellason

Cover design by pro_design37

Copyright Notices:

First Printing: 2025

ISBN: 979-8-9923902-4-7

Dr. Joan Weathersbee Ellason is available to provide workshops on forgiveness or other topics.

For booking information: Call or text (469) 831-4548

Email: DrJWE@outlook.com

Include WORKSHOP in the subject line.

Images and graphics by:

Spiritual – Dove: OpenClipart, Vine: Clker-Free-Vector-Images, Heart: Glyndwrgirl, Hug: Bianca Robben-van Dijk, Solitude under tree: GDJ, Rose: Erbs55, Hand in hand: Skalekar1992, Teardrop - OpenClipart-Vectors, Heart halves – Manuchi.

Appreciation is expressed to:

Ita de Groot, editor

Payal Renu, cover designer

Table of Contents

To the Reader

———————— ⟳ ————————

This book is to be read slowly and repeatedly. Pick it up as often as you like.

While the book and its works are copyrighted, the reader is allowed to use additional personal words that may enhance their personal meaning. For example, a meadow may not appeal to some readers, in which case, when reading it aloud or in their mind, the reader can verbally replace "meadow" with "forest" or "beach." Use the images that will be more beneficial to you during your contemplation readings.

These chapters are written by a Christian. It is

understood and hoped that people of all faiths and all walks of life will benefit from these pages and find strength from the one who created them.

Enjoy . . . .

My Testimony

———————— ❧ ————————

There was a time when I experienced a greater loss than I had ever imagined. I had plans. I was focused, striving toward my goals. Then, all at once, everything that I had trusted on the Earth was ripped out from under me. There was an effort to completely destroy everything that I had lived for. I felt betrayed, abandoned, and left without support from all of the human resources on which I had placed my hopes.

When what you believe to be the worst that could ever happen to you happens, where do you turn?

These pages are contemplations that I learned as I walked through an unprecedented valley in my life. I had been taught about God, taught to worship and follow Jesus, but until your whole world gets turned upside down and no one is there to help you in a tangible way—it is not until then that you ever get a chance to see up close, face-to-face, and palpably what really exists in the Heavenly realm that is and has always been there for you. It is here, when the tangible on Earth fails, that the Spiritual can show itself to be more real and available than Earthly resources ever could. When all I had left was God, I began to see how true, personal, and present for you and me He really is. Until then I had not learned the depth and realness of this Divine Love and Power.

These writings emerged from the juncture of my devastation and being left with nothing—the only thing remaining that I had was the hand of God. These writings are examples of what God showed me, contemplations that lifted me up above all that had happened, and I learned how profound, how real, and how specifically personal this resource, God, truly is for you and me.

Through these pages, I wish and pray for you to know the true realness of a profound love and power that exists as a constant that is personally and patiently available for you. When we tap into this resource, yes, the traditional God, Jesus, His Holy Spirit, I have come to learn that you and I can be lifted above and beyond whatever happens to us. We can see more than what merely meets the mortal eye.

Read any or all of these contemplations as you find relevant in your life. We have a true higher power that I have come to experience as one who loves us more than any parent or partner ever could, surpasses all that we can imagine, and is here with us continually. While I was taught about a traditional belief in God, Jesus, and His Holy Spirit, God showed me a reality far beyond what I had learned. He showed me how to become buffered, protected, and strengthened to rise above the turmoil and pain of this Earth.

It is hoped that you also launch into a greater, real, and tangible connection with the God who made you, sees you, knows you, deeply loves you, and has a good plan for your life.

Please use these writings to tap into the abundantly powerful, loving resource that is continuously there, patiently waiting for you to just simply reach up and connect.

You are not alone and do not have to go through challenges in life without this Higher Power who is with you and loves you more than you know.

"For I am convinced that neither death, nor life, nor angels, nor rulers, nor things present, nor things to come, nor powers, nor height, nor depth, nor anything else in all creation will be able to separate us from the love of God in Christ Jesus our Lord."

Romans 8:38-39 (NRSV)

Letter from God to You

————— ⌖ —————

"The Lord, your God, is in your midst,
a warrior who gives victory;
he will rejoice over you with gladness;
he will renew you in his love;
he will exult over you with loud singing."

Zephaniah 3:17 (NRSV)

My Dear Child,

You are not alone. You do not have to walk through these things in life all by yourself. I am with you every moment. *I AM ON YOUR SIDE*. How I wish you knew how deeply I love you!

You have been uniquely created by me, and I see you as Beautiful. I am SO PROUD of YOU!

As you walk through the ups and downs, twists and turns of life, I want you to know that I am HERE. When so many things do not go the way you had hoped, I want you to know that I have fashioned a better way for you. I have good plans for you, for your life—even if you cannot see that just yet.

I can give you more strength than you ever imagined possible. You are my precious child whom I have loved from the foundation of the world. I knew you even before you were born, and I have placed you upon the Earth at exactly the right and perfect time. You are designed as a blessing to the world, and in your very existence, you are a profound blessing to Me.

It is my great desire to be allowed to make your life better. I will do this *only* with your permission.

"Behold, I stand at the door and knock. If anyone hears My voice and opens the door, I will come in to him and dine with him, and he with Me."

Revelation 3:20 (NKJV)

Your life has meaning and has a purpose, even when to you it may seem impossible. Please allow me to show this to you.

Know that I will never leave you nor forsake you. *I will fight for you. I will rescue you. I will defend you.*

I LOVE YOU more than you could ever imagine!

Contemplation One:
You Are Not Alone

"Can a mother forget the baby at her breast
and have no compassion on the child she has
borne?
Though she may forget,
I will not forget you!
See, I have engraved you on the palms of my hands;
your walls are ever before me."

Isaiah 49: 15–16 (NIV)

Do you know how *truly* loved you are? Each moment and every second of every day, even if someone has left you or rejected you, that has not decreased one fraction of the profound love that the Creator of the Universe has for you.

Take a deep breath. Did you see any of the oxygen

go into your lungs right now? Did it nurture your body? Yes. It is here as a constant and nurtures your body—only if you breathe it in. Take a moment now and breathe in the Love that is here as a constant, right now for you.

You are walking in a meadow with thick, rich, green grass. The sun is shining with warmth. You feel it caressing your cheeks, and the breeze blows gently through your hair. As you walk, your feet are cushioned and cradled with soft, rich green grass—so soft that you are able to walk barefoot. In this place you can find peace and comfort.

Notice the safety in this place. You see a nearby tree standing tall, strong, and sturdy. Allow yourself to sit upon the soft green grass beneath it and to lean back against its strong, sturdy trunk. As you rest here comfortably, in your mind's eye you begin to see the Creator of the Universe, who is with you and has been with you through the most difficult times. In your mind's eye, you look up, and you see Jesus sitting face-to-face in front of you, gazing into your eyes with a love that goes far beyond any love that you have ever experienced here on Earth—ever. You begin to realize that the warm sun you felt was actually Him caressing your cheeks and adoring you. As you look up into your Creator's eyes, you begin to feel a river of love that flows deep into your heart and deep into your soul.

Allow yourself to breathe in this love. For you are not alone. This is a place of retreat for you to rest and replenish your strength at any time that you need to feel safe.

As you continue to rest in this place, you begin to notice a sense of security. You feel warmth all around you, like a blanket of love that cradles you. For you are wrapped up in the arms of God, safe, peaceful, secure, and Loved for the very one you are. Allow yourself to tune in to this feeling of God's mighty arms wrapped around you so securely. Rest here for a while.

In a moment you may begin to hear the gentle voice of the one who created you, knows you, and loves you, saying reassuringly to you,

"You are safe with me. I am here. I will never leave you nor forsake you. I have loved you throughout all your life. I am with you and will never leave you.

"Breathe in this warmth, safety, and love. Allow

this to fill up your heart and soul. Rest. Recharge. Renew. Return to this place as often as you need to. Remember that you, oh precious one, are not alone."

Contemplation Two:
Realizing the Truth of Your Value

—————— ⚬⚭ ——————

"For you created my inmost being;
you knit me together in my mother's womb.
I praise you because

I am fearfully and wonderfully made;
your works are wonderful,
I know that full well."

Psalms 139:13–14 (NIV)

Far above in the Heavens, as a beautiful soul persisted in the mind of the Creator of the Universe forever, it was *finally* the time to bring this lovely unique one into fruition.

Allow yourself to look up into the Heavens now and visualize this scene that took place about your beginnings. You can take a glimpse into the planning and origins of the very one you are.

"*Yes*, it is *finally* the time!" the Creator said with excitement. "Bring in your BEST features, for THIS one will be *SO* amazing!"

All the Heavens gathered around with excitement and anticipation at the new unique work that was about to emerge. As God spoke, you could hear the words booming across the heavens. "This child will be replicated by no one, surpassed by none, and unlike anyone who came before."

You watch as an image is formed, spanning all ages of development from inception and across the whole entire lifespan. Allow yourself to witness this front-row seat and unique insight into the creation of . . . YOU.

As you watch the Highest Power of the Universe surge with glee and delight, you see and hear God's distinct orders with such detail and specification ring out through the Heavens that those gathering around sigh with amazement and anticipation. Every detail, down to the fingerprints and hair color, even to the tiniest microscopic cell and DNA, is outlined in a blueprint that is only and uniquely for you. You hear a command of talents and gifts being designed. Some will remain dormant until it is time for their development, at which point they can blossom and grow. Those in the Heavens cheer on this new and amazing one-of-a-kind creation that is YOU.

Now, you also hear a very unexpected addition to this work of art. "We will also apply some features that will serve as hidden gifts. These will come to be understood at a later time and will be seen by some humans as flaws, annoyances, or weaknesses. Yet from the midst of these will emerge even greater gifts and strengths that confound their understanding." This mix of perfection with perceived imperfection is at the very core of this work of genius.

You hear the wisdom of the Great Teacher who has formed this specific formula that is you—and uniquely you alone. The Creator says to those up in Heaven who look onward, "Some of these hidden gifts will save this person's life one day. Others will serve to steer them in the direction of a higher purpose that they would otherwise miss. Yet even more of these hidden gifts that humans may perceive as flaws will launch this person into the brilliance and insight that they would otherwise fail to see."

Now, as you see the finished creation—You—you can turn up the volume and make the scene you witness above more clearly vivid. Cheers are ringing throughout the Heavens with roaring applause. Surrounded by all this celebration, as the Creator now holds you and looks you deeply in the eye, you begin to feel the security of God's strong arms around you, holding you up, and you can see and feel a profound depth of Love pouring into your heart. You notice as the cheering noise in the background fades, that this one—the Highest Power—is so intently enthralled in the beauty and uniqueness of you that for this moment, this appears to be the only moment that exists.

Everything stands still and falls into quiet background around you and the Creator. You are able to witness face–to–face the fact that you are wrapped up in the arms of God. You become filled with a pure and powerful gaze of amazement and love that is being poured directly into your heart from the eyes and heart of God—especially for you. You are loved and cherished uniquely, specifically.

From the moment of your beginnings, this gaze has never left your face, not even for one moment, not even at your worst. You still are and remain the apple of God's eye, uniquely filled with purpose and love, created as a brilliant masterpiece.

Contemplation Three:
Getting Rid of Turmoil and Stress
An Oasis Part I

———— ❧ ————

"He makes me lie down in green pastures,
he leads me beside quiet waters,
He refreshes my soul.
He guides me along the right paths
for his name's sake."

Psalms 23:2–3 (NIV)

Come away from the noise. Let's get away from
everything for just a few moments.

As you walk peacefully through a quiet, serene meadow, you begin to feel a cool breeze gently wash across your whole entire being. Perhaps you sit or choose to lie back, feeling yourself surrounded with soft green grass and the blissful scent of fresh flowers and tall trees. You begin to hear the faint sound of a nearby brook as its water gently flows, washing and cleansing away all the former stress. Now the noise quietens.

The breeze in this place soothes your soul and quietens your mind as you begin to tune in to its uniquely restful aroma. As you look up, you see that a gently loving light is reaching from the Highest Heavenly place, directly from the Hand of God to you—personally. Take a moment to notice the unique blend of hope, peace, and holiness that God is supplying to you right now through this light. Breathe in its unique aroma filled with love and compassion for you. This is specifically for you right now.

All else fades into oblivion as you begin to focus only on the present senses in this place. Allow yourself to notice its unique color and soothing aroma, specifically blended together to meet your needs right now. As your Loving Creator knows *exactly* what you need right now, allow yourself to notice its specific hues, aromas, and texture. Is it sweet? Is it light? Is its texture soft? Perhaps it feels thick and comforting like a warm blanket of protection. Notice that God, who knows exactly what you need at this moment, orchestrates the exact blend of comforting hues, scents, and strengths to nurture you right where you are with exactly what you need. Take a deep breath and breathe in this specific antidote supplied just for you—for what you need at this very moment. Allow yourself to become filled with these ingredients from someone who loves you and knows you in a way that no one else can.

Take all the time you need here. With each breath, you become filled with a new sense of rest, peace, emotional security, and renewed strength.

Getting Rid of Turmoil and Stress
An Oasis Part II

———— ❧ ————

"I will exalt you, Lord,
for you lifted me out of the depths
and did not let my enemies gloat over me."

Psalms 30: 1 (NIV)

Come away from the noise. Let's get away and rise
above everything. In the twinkling of a moment, you
can become lifted up and soar above the chaos.

As you step outside for a moment, you allow the door to close behind you like a final blow, pushing back against all the chaos that was inside.

You step barefoot out onto a meadow. Feel the soft grass beneath your feet. You look up and notice the warmth of the sun inviting you to come away, almost as if it is calling you to experience a new oasis of retreat. You feel drawn to a feeling of freedom . . . peace . . . . safety. Notice the smell of clean air as a gentle breeze softly caresses your cheeks. The sun warms your heart like a blanket of love.

As you look up, the clouds begin to take the shape of the face of a loving Creator smiling gently back at you.

You notice in the distance, anchored and waiting for you, a beautiful hot-air balloon with such an intricate blend of colors that it brightens your spirit the moment you lay eyes upon it. It is there waiting for you—waiting to lift you up out of the noise and the pressure, allowing you to float away from the demands.

You approach it and notice its strength. You feel the solid texture of its basket. You can see clearly that it is safe, secure, and anchored to the ground.

You climb into the strong, sturdy basket and allow yourself to lift the rope that was holding it down. You begin to float gently up at a slow and gentle pace.

For the moment, you are only a few feet above the ground. You can stay at this level if you so desire. As you look down in this basket that securely holds you, you notice some sandbags at your feet.

You look closer and see that each one has a label, titles of stressors and pressures. Look down for a moment at a particularly small sandbag. As you read its label, it represents one of your smaller stressors. Reach down, feel it. Perhaps it is rough and is an inconvenience to you. Pick it up and, with a mighty arm, hurl it out of the basket as far as you can throw it! Immediately, you feel lifted up ever so slightly.

Notice another sandbag. Perhaps this one represents a bigger pressure—a demand that you have not been able to get rid of. Now, with even more strength, reach down, pick it up, and with all your might, hurl it over the edge of the balloon's basket. With this one, as you throw it over the edge, it makes a sound as it impacts the ground. Ah…. now you are able to float up, feeling much, much lighter than before. The balloon rises and takes you to a new height. Freer. Lighter. Higher. And still so very safe and secure.

Continue taking each sandbag, one by one, freeing

the space around your now unencumbered feet—throwing each one out of the balloon and out of your life. With each sandbag labeled and representing some burden of some type, you become more lifted, lighter, and freer when you see it hurtling toward the Earth below—never to burden you again.

Now you are floating free, sailing through the air. Light and carefree. You look up and see the clouds appear to form the shape of a smiling face, as sunshine bursts through the edges of the cloud formations as if God is radiating warmth toward you and embracing you from above.

Allow yourself to stay in this place for as long as you need to. As you float above all the world's cares, you feel lighter, freer. Take a nice deep breath of this fresh air up here—here where all is free and light. As you soar above all the chaos below, the sounds below are muted, silenced, and have no more power over you. Every one of the stressors are now just tiny little sandbags lying on the ground far below. They look so tiny from where you are. Allow yourself to maintain this snapshot of their tininess—their minuscule insignificance. As you soar above, you feel the freedom of a beautiful breeze gently blowing through your hair and the warm sun caressing your cheeks, the gentle hand of God nourishing you. Remain in this place for as long as you need.

When you are ready, you can return, slowly moving closer back toward the ground. As you look, you notice a very funny thing happening. As you get closer to the ground, each sandbag shrinks even further. Now they are no more than powerless, tiny little inanimate objects below your feet.

Gradually, you gently land upon the meadow of soft grass. The loving warmth of the sun remains with you, and you land lighter, freer, and unencumbered.

You can return here anytime you need—anytime you need to shut the door to the chaos. You can reduce the stressors into tiny little objects that no longer have impact.

Contemplation Four:
An Oasis Away from the Chaos
When Overwhelmed

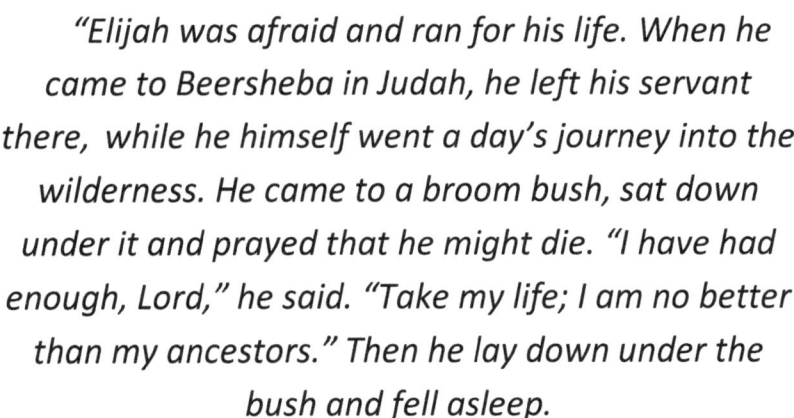

"Elijah was afraid and ran for his life. When he came to Beersheba in Judah, he left his servant there, while he himself went a day's journey into the wilderness. He came to a broom bush, sat down under it and prayed that he might die. "I have had enough, Lord," he said. "Take my life; I am no better than my ancestors." Then he lay down under the bush and fell asleep.

All at once an angel touched him and said, "Get up and eat." He looked around, and there by his head was some bread baked over hot coals, and a jar of water. He ate and drank and then lay down again.

The angel of the Lord came back a second time

and touched him and said, "Get up and eat, for the journey is too much for you." So he got up and ate and drank. Strengthened by that food, he traveled forty days and forty nights until he reached Horeb, the mountain of God."

1 Kings 19: 3–8 (NIV)

You are standing on a mountain surrounded by dark and cold. This is a mountain that you have climbed a million times. It seems to go on forever. You are surrounded by a dull, rank smell. The further you go, the more rocks and barriers you see. Your feet are bleeding, and your skin feels grimy from this long, treacherous journey. It seems like it will never end. Why do I keep hitting these roadblocks? I am doing all the work—no one is helping. No one understands. No one cares. This is just too much—too much to bear! You are overwhelmed.

With your fists clenched and raised, you scream with a shriek that shakes the heavens around you. **WHY? WHY?**

You begin to notice through the darkness a glimmering, flickering light; small at first, almost too tiny to see. It begins to pierce through the darkness. Then, ever so gently, it reaches toward you as if to say, "I see you. You are not alone. I am here."

It grows, becoming brighter as it gently reaches with warmth toward you like a ray of hope from out of nowhere. Its ever-growing warmth gently expands and emerges brighter and warmer as it directly enters this place. All at once, it begins to vanquish the darkness and eradicate that negative, odorous atmosphere as it flows. You begin to smell the sweet, fresh aroma of fresh, clean air. With it comes a unique and loving mixture of lavender, vanilla, rose, and jasmine. Take a nice deep breath and notice how with each breath you begin to release and let go of all that had been troubling you.

With its warmth and powerful gentleness, it begins to embrace your body and soul as a loving blanket of peace, love, and tranquility. With a kind and soothing voice, you begin to hear the words of the one who created you begin to say, "Come away with me, even if just for a moment." A momentary escape from stress . . . An oasis to replenish, renew, and recharge. Gently, softly, you hear the words, "Let go of the turmoil even if just for a few moments become wrapped up in Hope .... Peace .... *LOVE*.

All at once, as with a gentle breeze, you are lifted and transported to a higher place up above the turmoil that was below. Time stands still now. In this moment, all on Earth can wait as you are lifted above the chaos below. Now, you are cradled in the arms of God. You hear soft, sweet music, gentle and soothing tones that bring you back to happier times—times of peace and unfettered bliss, times of safety. Replenish and refresh your soul with the soothing touch of Heavenly warmth and serenity. In this moment—in the Here and Now—all is quiet. All is peaceful. All is safe. All the noise and cacophony of demands below become faint, smaller, until they fade away into a muted abyss of nothingness. You are cradled in the arms of your creator, and nothing else matters right now.

As you breathe in the fresh aroma of God's Love, let it replenish your soul and quieten your mind. Notice the mixture of lavender, vanilla, rose, and jasmine all intertwined into a symphony of peace and quietness. Take another slow, deep breath and allow this place to replenish your heart and soul. Tune in with all five senses. Feel the gentle touch of your Creator's warmth and the aroma of the fresh air filling your lungs, replenishing your heart and soul. Connect with the beauty of this loving place. You are wrapped up in light and warmth. Notice the colors that you see. Breathe in the sense of serenity and peace. Hear in the midst of the quietness the soft, soothing sound of Divine Love replenishing you with words of hope— specifically and personally for you.

"I am with you."

"The chaos can wait."

"You can rest here."

"You will get through this."

"You are stronger than you think you are."

You are smarter than you think you are."

"You do not have to go through this alone."

"I am with you and will help you."

As you allow yourself to remain here for as long as you need to, time stands still. Take as much time as you need.

Retreat here as often as you can and for as long as needed, just as the angels ministered to Elijah. He rested, slept, awoke to receive nourishment, and slept again. Then he returned to the mountain greatly strengthened.

Contemplation Five:
Gentle Beauty: Aging Lovingly

———— ✐ ————

"Even to your old age and gray hairs
I am he, I am he who will sustain you.
I have made you and I will carry you;
I will sustain you and I will rescue you."

Isaiah 46:4 (NIV)

The image in the mirror has changed into something difficult to recognize.

What has happened?

The hair is thin . . . everything has changed.

Now, realizing that the pace has slowed, it takes longer to heal when injured. The nightstand is now filled with various prescriptions, supplements, and pain creams.

In these moments, as you are beginning to learn the challenge of patience with yourself, much more grace is required. Grace for the slowing of activity, the preserving of energy. Naps have now become a lovely, welcome respite before work can be completed—right in the middle of the day. A nap is now a luxury.

Sometimes memory is not your friend. Things do not come as easy as they did before. No longer can you lift heavy objects but have to rely on someone younger, stronger, more capable. Multitasking and technology may now feel stressful or overwhelming.

To your greatest chagrin, people are now doing more and more things for you, as you feel your grip of independence slipping further away into embarrassment, resentment, and humiliation. So easy to resent this! What's next? The car keys? What other freedoms?

But this experience of helplessness and dependency is not new. This is not the first time life has been this way.

You look up in front of you and see a large TV screen. There was another time when you had to take things slowly; another time when people had to do almost everything for you. There was another point in your life when fast pacing and too much at a time was overwhelming. You easily became overstimulated. Let's look at a time when life was this way before. How decidedly we experience amnesia for such a time as this was in our lives!

Look above at the giant movie screen right before your eyes. There are wails and cries, or perhaps this is peaceful.

All at once, the tiniest, most helpless being emerges from the womb.

It is You.

Others are standing around in amazement at the miraculous masterpiece that has just emerged onto the planet—You—a precious gift, a brand-new wonderful bundle of joy. There may have been a loving welcoming committee of enamored eyes beaming upon you and arms waiting to hold you. Or there may have been a different set of circumstances, but make no mistake, there was a chorus of loving Angels cheering your entry. Allow yourself for a moment to focus on this loving celebration, whether it came from the people near you or from Angels above. God has placed you here, and there is joy at your arrival. You were meant to be here.

Focus on the loving eyes of God, angels, and loving caretakers you remember. Parents? Grandparents? Aunts? Other male or female relatives?

Now, on the screen, you can see from the Heavens a warm, loving, gentle stream of light shining down upon this tiny little being—You. You notice that this magnificent light is wrapping you in its love like a gentle blanket of protection all around you.

Allow yourself to move as much as you wish into this scene shown on this screen. You may even choose, for a BRIEF moment, to literally slip into this little one being born. Slip back into the You that was at that time. Let yourself feel the amazement of this stage of life. You begin to feel the loving, warm light of protection around you and the admiring faces marveling at your tender state.

Feeling the warm light of welcoming love that is coming from your Creator, you begin to hear a gentle voice saying to you, "Welcome to the world, my precious one, my lovely. You have been the apple of my eye from before the moment of your conception. You are my pride and joy. You are beautiful."

What you see on this movie screen is a metamorphosis of beauty. The tiny little infant is completely helpless and requires the help of those around who are more capable, stronger, more adept. The precious little infant is to be treated with much more gentleness, tenderness, patience, and grace than the rest of the human race that rushes by. This need for help continues as you grow.

Notice that this stage of dependence is expected, honored, and welcomed.

As you revisit this stage of your life, you begin to realize that after many decades of living, pursuing challenges, and overcoming so many obstacles, a return to a position of honor, tenderness, gentleness, and patience with yourself is exactly what is merited.

You had strength outwardly and now your strength is transformed inwardly. Notice your internal strengths—wisdom, experience, knowledge, and endurance from decades on Earth. These years of hard-earned wisdom and depth determine and deserve a return to a stage of preciousness and tenderness. Consider this time of your life as a time to treat yourself as a beautiful, exquisite, and valuable being. You are no longer required to run recklessly through the night, conquer foes with Herculean strength, or trample over mountains. That is for others to do now. You have more than earned this permission, prerogative, and benefit.

As you ponder these things, you may wish to bring the image of the infant that is You, back to where you now sit. Allow yourself to see *this* You in the mirror with fresh eyes. You look up and see light coming from above as it flows toward you and begins to embrace you with profound love and honor. This is You—a veteran survivor of so many things. You are still that same tender, amazing miracle—now with a well-earned legacy.

If ready, allow yourself to reach out and draw this precious being close to your heart—this YOU who has spent so much—a long life with so many endeavors. So many sacrifices and battles you have fought for so many, and, even if just only for you, you have fought them well and with the scars to prove it, worn proudly like badges of honor and bravery. So long overdue, wrap yourself in a blanket of honor. Wrap your arms around this little being—You—who has now arrived back full circle to a state of preciousness and honor at the age that you are now. Allow yourself to extend love and honor for the very one you are. Wrap up this lovely You with a warm, soft blanket of respect and honor. This is a time to treat yourself with dignity and gentleness, respect and tenderness, love and hopefulness.

As you lay in bed tonight, remember that you are still that wonderful gift of awe and wonder. You are still that miracle, as you begin to celebrate everything that you still *CAN* do, even if with more diligent, deliberate pacing. Allow yourself to see the present You in this new light.

Now, as you see yourself walk, you can see your current slow pace as one with an important purpose.

Slow, deliberate moves are specifically focused on protecting this long-lived amazing body that has endured so much and is now to be respected. Your entire being is infused with honor and dignity, as you treat yourself with care and respect. You lovingly adorn yourself each day with honor. You move through life with patience, intentionality, and tenderness toward every facet of your being as the precious one that you are—created by God.

Contemplation Six: From Shattered to Surpassed

Rising Above

———— ✑ ————

"He who was seated on the throne said, "I am making everything new!" Then he said, "Write this down, for these words are trustworthy and true."

Revelation 21:5 (NIV)

Standing there, with a million pieces of your life broken around you at your feet, you look upon each piece of your dream... your plans... your life... your hopes. You notice something not seen before . . . that each piece of your dream, your life, and your innocence is still here. Every bit of it. Take a minute to see and acknowledge this.

Each and every piece of your dream is still there waiting for you; YOU the artist, the composer of what You can become. You feel your tears pour onto these scattered pieces as it now seems to be a collage of broken hopes and dreams in devastating disarray. Pour out your tears. Let them flow. As a river, they wash over this tapestry of pieces. Each piece is relevant. Each piece is precious. Each piece remaining—all of them. You notice as you look out over what now seems to be a disordered and chaotic collage of images that each piece still remains. Though broken, each and every piece still remains present in your life, just in a different form, waiting for its re-creation. Nothing has been wasted.

Allow your tears to wash over them as they cleanse, restore, and renew them. Each tear becomes a polishing varnish for even the tiniest of the shattered pieces—no matter how small. Nothing has been wasted. Everything you have poured into this hope—your time, your energy, your dedication, your trust, everything that you invested—has not been wasted. You begin to see that more is yet to come out of this.

As your tears continue to pour out onto each part of your dream, each piece becomes illuminated, gradually reshaped. Each still has its intended purpose and awaits an unprecedented transformation. As you look upon each piece of your dream, you notice that each and every part—each one—is essential to the creation of a new masterpiece. Washing over this with tears is a vital part of this process. Allow yourself time for this, the cleansing of what was not, to allow a new space for what can emerge.

Time stands still and awaits patiently for you to take as long as you need, tenderly cleansing each precious piece of your dream as your tears wash over them. Allow yourself to hear truths from Heaven. You begin to hear the soft, loving voice of your Creator speak in such a gentle voice these truths:

"Nothing has been wasted. I will take all these pieces and bring them together into a new creation—a new tapestry of your life that goes beyond anything that you have ever imagined. All is still here. Nothing is ultimately lost; it just takes on a new form. Your love for that person. Your generous and loving effort poured into that person, plan, dream becomes transformed."

As you continue to hear the words from above, you can hear it almost like that of a rushing mighty wind that at the same time is for you a gentle, loving breeze. You may notice an array of beautiful colors that form around the voice of your loving Creator. Allow yourself to tune in fully to its sounds, colors, aromas, and physical soothing flow as it gently wraps you in protection.

Allow yourself to become fully focused upon this soothing, healing voice of your protective Creator as you continue to hear more truths. You now begin to see the profound reality that no person on Earth—no human being—has the power nor the authority to take away *ANYTHING* that God has given to you. That child, that spouse, your innocence—everything given to you by God still remains and resides in your heart.

Behold, I make all things new again. I will take all these pieces and restore all of them into a new pattern, where your life rises above all that has happened, and you begin to walk on a new level. You will soon begin to see what your Heavenly Creator can make out of all these pieces.

You now begin to notice that all your efforts spent on this dream begin to become intertwined with the touch of your Creator in a magnificent blend that becomes more vibrant and powerful than ever before. New colors and hues emerge that surpass anything ever experienced here on this Earth with just human art alone. Now each and every piece begins to rise up and transform into a new configuration—an immense collage of purpose—a new masterpiece. Each piece remains and is not lost. Each piece having a new position on this amazing tapestry of your life. Notice how you can allow these pieces to transform their place and meaning. With each day, all the elements of your former dream give way to a brand-new creation—little by little, day by day—until all is transformed into its proper place. Justice is restored. Healing is realized.

Give yourself all the time that you need for this process; knowing that all your energy, time, love, effort, and purpose remain fully and completely intact.

"And I will restore to you the years that the locust hath eaten, the cankerworm, and the caterpillar, and the palmerworm, my great army which I sent among you.

And ye shall eat in plenty, and be satisfied, and praise the name of the Lord your God, that hath dealt wondrously with you: and my people shall never be ashamed."

Joel 2:25–26 (KJV)

Contemplation Seven:

Part I

My Child, Now Out of Reach

"No parent should ever have to bury a child."

Lou Weathersbee, my mother

Why? . . . . . Why? . . . . WHY???

If only I could hold you forever.

You were—you *ARE*—my miracle—my pride and joy—my precious child—forever.

If only I could have prevented what happened! I had so many plans and dreams for you, for your life. It is so hard to let go of them—of YOU!

I will NEVER let you go! I want to see you again . . . NOW. I can't bear this separation.

Will this grief never end?

As you sit by the window and look out into the night sky, you see the stars above. Take a moment to imagine that you have a unique ability to see clearly across the universe and into the Heavens. As you know, as true as the stars are in the sky, your child is just across the way.

As you sit and peer across the universe, a river of love flows from your heart with an eternally unbroken connection that reaches that precious one. No one—nothing—can break the bond of a parent to a child. It remains permanent, solid, unshakable, and unstoppable. Feel the sense of this secure and enduring energy as it continues to maintain a strong connection to your loved one.

While in life that child may have at times just been in the next room or only separated by a small barrier such as the womb, life and death have not changed that. Your bond with them remains connected forever.

As you look through this window, you begin to see the love from your heart take tangible form. It begins to feel solid and strong. You see and feel it connecting directly from your heart across the entire universe, reaching all the way to your child. Feel it now, as your heart reaches across the heavens into the next room, where your child is resting peacefully in God's arms. As you feel the matchless, powerful river of the love in your heart, you can see how it extends all of the way into the Heavens and begins to wrap gently around your child like an eternal blanket of motherly/fatherly connection that will never be broken—ever. Notice the depth of your emotion transform into a flow of energy that is able to reach and soothe your precious one right now, wherever they are at this very moment. Notice that you are STILL their mother/father.

All at once, you are able to see much more in that opening through the Heavens. There is a glistening, bright, illuminating light that emanates throughout the sky. As you look through this prism of light, you can see peace and safety embracing your child. Notice that You can see a glimpse of your child being held, cradled, and protected by God's loving arms. You are able to see up close a profoundly peaceful expression on your child's face. In this dimension, you are able to connect without words. You are able to learn that your child is safe and also that your child knows that they will see you again. Knowing that in Heaven, days, months, and years are but as brief moments.

This is a brief moment of separation, as they are just in the next room, and you will be reunited again someday. As the Angels are caring for your child, you are reminded that they still have your love, and you have theirs. Your connection of love is a powerful, fervent, and unstoppable force that remains solid and secure forever.

Contemplation Seven:

Part II

Loss of a Parent

——————— ✆ ——————— *

"When my father and my mother forsake me,
Then the Lord will take care of me."

Psalm 27:10 (NKJV)

You were—*ARE* supposed to be—my anchor to the earth—the one I check in with—go to for safety—lean on for refuge—*Mom? Dad?* I have never envisioned a day without you alive—somewhere—in which I could just call you and hear your voice whenever I need to. Even if I was busy and thought I didn't need you, I did. Even if you were not there perfectly for me, I still dreamt of one day things being better.

Now, it seems as if things can never be as they were supposed to be. Too late to repair. Too late to tell you what I wanted to say. I thought I had more time, but I didn't. How I wish I could have, would have, should have said those things to you.

Even if I was busy . . . perhaps distant . . . perhaps caught up in life—too busy to do enough for you—you were my anchor, and I felt some sense of security because you were here somewhere on the earth caring about me or praying for me. Even if you did not do things that I needed while on the earth or did not do enough, I still need you. I need you or even the fantasy of you being there for me like parents are supposed to be—eternally, with no end. I need what we didn't have or didn't have enough of:

time . . . amends . . . words . . . closeness . . . love.

Now I feel orphaned. It feels as if the safety net

is gone, even if it were not perfectly strong or present often enough. I need your comfort—your *LOVE*. Who can I go to? Who can I count on? Who on earth can care about me the way that you did, or were supposed to? If only I could call you on the phone, hear your voice one more time . . . reach out for help or advice once again.

No one can replace the love of a parent. No one can love me the way that a parent does or should— no spouse, no partner, not even a best friend. Who can replace Mom—Dad—Mother—Father?

Allow yourself to take a moment in the quiet of the night or perhaps the breeze of the day. Pull up a comforting memory of that parent. There may be many or very few of those moments. There may have only been the nine months in the womb, where you were fundamentally protected and buffered from the outside world. Allow yourself to sit with any of these memories that come to mind.

Every positive experience that you have had with that parent, many or few, wonderful or imperfect, lives on in your DNA and in the very core of your being, woven within the very fabric of your soul. It is like a beautiful tapestry of wonderful fabric that lives on in you and through you.

One positive memory can hold sustaining power to overcome and eradicate even the darkest of times. Connect with this memory.

Focus on that one central positive moment. Perhaps it is the time when that parent smiled at you or said those very needed and timely words of encouragement. Center your attention on that one single moment.

Now, make it more vivid. Turn up the volume. See the colors, feel the textures around you in that connection. Bring in the memory of any familiar soothing scents. Turn up the volume of that precious experience, regardless of how brief. Make it last longer than it originally was. Hold it suspended in time. Savor it. Hold it in your heart.

Our parents' positive strengths can have a unique way of lasting within us, long after that person has gone. People sometimes spend years of therapy trying to reduce the *un*wanted influences of their parents. Therefore, the positive strengths of your parents can likewise live on within you for as long as you need. You can connect with the positive features they poured into you and hold them in your heart continually.

Right now, begin to notice those positive strengths, influences, and personality features that you remember about them. Enhance them to the fullest. Spend time here. Replay their positive words in your mind. Allow yourself to rekindle that nurturance, whether it was received often or not often enough. Regardless, one ounce of strength, one positive and meaningful moment can live on and grow within you. Draw from them now.

Allow yourself to sit with these positive memories. Feel a blanket of warmth wrap around you as you tune in and fully connect with the maternal and paternal love that you have received. Bring in a memory of that pleasant moment—or perhaps an amusing one. Remember each one, one at a time. Savor this positive experience. Allow yourself to bring in your sensory experiences with these moments. You may now recall a positive aroma, their familiar voice, and the scenery and texture of a pleasant environment when you were with them. Turn up the volume and sit with these memories for as long as you need.

You can revisit these positive experiences often.

Remembering a time when that parent was just in the next room, their positive strengths never left you. As it was then, it can also be now. Their love remains with you. While you knew that their feet were planted somewhere on the earth, you continued to feel anchored, planted, grounded, and secure. Take that sense of strength and notice it. Feel this same foundation firmly fixed beneath your feet— the sense of a safety net still present, still intact. The love and connection to maternal and paternal love remain unbreakable.

Now, as you look deeper. . . . .

As you look beneath your feet in search of that parental safety net that you had always counted on, you begin to see something even stronger and more solid than you had perhaps ever noticed before.

Take a moment to see. As a mist begins to roll back the clouds at your feet, an image is gently coming into view. You begin to feel warmth, safety, and familiarity as the haze dissipates, creating a clearing.

You begin to notice that this is something even more solid than perhaps what you had seen before. It is stronger than all of the tangible elements on earth on which you placed your dependence and faith. Allow yourself to look deeper to see something that has been there all along.

You begin to realize that you are not alone, that you are not orphaned, and that you have actually never been without a safety net. In the clearing, you begin to see a constant and permanent foundation that has been there throughout all your life, in good experiences and bad.

You begin to feel its resilience and strength holding you up. It has been supporting you for all your life—through even the hardest of experiences. Now, though your parent is as if they are in the next room and not present with you in the same way as before, you can allow yourself to become more aware of this perhaps overlooked but stronger foundation that is supporting you. It has always been there.

Allow the sensation of your feet making contact with the Hand of God. Feel the sense of being firmly planted on solid ground. Notice its stability and that it is immovable. You may imagine walking or even jumping up and down upon its supportive structure. Notice your solid footing.

This acquaintance is actually not new. For this was the foundation from which you began, before any parents, siblings, friends, or loved ones came into your life. You begin to realize that God was the original First Parent before the parents whom you were given.

All your life, you have been held up, supported, and sheltered by the Hand of God. It has always been there and will always remain with you, under your feet as your anchor, foundation, and place to land.

Allow yourself to feel the sensation of being firmly planted and secure upon this foundation. Connect with this source of strength for as long as you need. Revisit it as often as you need.

Know that it has always been there and is always with you. You continually remain wrapped up in the Love and Arms of God. You remain firmly and steadfastly supported by the Hand of God.

Contemplation Eight:
What is Wrong with Them??!!

"...Now I know in part; then I shall know fully,
even as I am fully known."

1 Corinthians 13:12 (NIV)

The opposing person . . . that politician . . . that rebellious child . . . *WHY??? WHY* do they do the things they do?

WHY do they think that way?? Whoever they are . . . we are going to imagine a video of their life.

Sit quietly in a safe, comfortable place. Shut out all

noise. Set your technology on "Do not disturb." We are going to observe and explore behind the eyes of our opponent, naysayer, enemy, or just that person who is different that we don't understand. Albeit through imagery and only what we imagine could be, we are going to allow ourself to see what is more than meets the eye.

Visualize them at a distance in front of you. You can see them, but they cannot see you.

Now construct any boundaries that you need. You can imagine one of your own making. Notice it. Notice its thickness, how sturdy it is… its strength. Take your hand and run it across its texture and feel that it is *absolutely* solid. Take your time to let your fingers touch it. Scan over the surface, feeling the strength and solidity of this boundary between you and that person.

You begin to hear their voice. Is it ranting? Yelling? Shouting? Or is it whispering? There is a small panel in front of you with a volume knob. As you reach out and put your fingers on the knob, you begin to turn it. As you turn the knob, you notice that you can lower the volume of their voice. As you continue to turn the knob, this noise becomes lower, lower, lower, until it is completely gone and all is quiet.

Bring in this quietness as it becomes bigger, more quiet . . . bigger and tangible, like a thick, soothing blanket that gently fills the room and softly embraces you and wraps around your shoulders. You can feel its safety all at once and begin to notice a fragrant aroma emanating from this wonderful, quiet, soothing, soft protection—one that reminds you of a time when you felt very safe. Take a moment to reconnect with a memory of a time when you were safe, protected, and sheltered. Remember the aroma from that earlier time and bring it into the present here and now. Take a moment to breathe in its wonderful aroma, as it soothes you from the top of your head to the bottom of your toes and the tips of your fingers.

This will be an important buffer for you and a protection for the next steps on our journey.

As you look at the person on the other side of that boundary you constructed, you notice that they are now quiet, still, and completely unaware of you at all. While you are fully enveloped, secure, and wrapped in the blanket of quietness, you can be positioned to see a glimpse behind their eyes.

Now, while you are gently wrapped up in the blanket of soothing quietness and protection, allow yourself to slowly become teleported upward. As you begin to float above the boundary, you feel safer and lighter as you rise. As you move to their side of that boundary, they remain unaware of your presence, and you remain buffered and fully wrapped up in that soothing blanket of protection.

Now you are able to see from a position behind them, as if through their own eyes. As you notice the movie screen in front of you, still at a safe distance, you can begin to see some of their life experiences. Adjust the distance, clarity, and volume so that you are now able to see a glimpse of their own internal world and perception. You are able to see what you need to see while still remaining totally buffered and protected from them. Everything you see on that movie screen is adjustable and controlled by you. Notice how different from yours their internal world appears.

All at once, you notice a vast difference in this atmosphere behind their eyes and possibly a faint odor that is foreign to you. You remain cushioned from all the elements in this environment as you take a closer look into their internal world. Again the small panel appears in front of you, and you notice that it has even more knobs and dials than before, allowing you to have full control over how much you allow yourself to see. This time you can adjust the images to be closer or farther away, larger or smaller, and you can choose what channels you wish to see. The amazing protective blanket of quietness continues to keep you separated from this person's internal world with a solid boundary, allowing you to see safely all that you wish to see about their own perceptions and interpretations while completely buffered and protected.

You select one of the channels. Perhaps their childhood? Perhaps their adult experiences? Perhaps their own thought process as you can imagine it to be. Knowing that we all as humans have the sanctity of boundary over our own mind and that we cannot actually know for certain the details in another's mind or world, we can imagine what may be likely. What may have formed their inexplicable opinions?

Select one of the channels and allow yourself to see a video clip of what may have influenced their thinking. Perhaps the earliest time when it all got started. What might have made them so adamant, so deeply entrenched, so dogmatic, so stubborn? Take as much time as you need.

As you tune into their internal world as you can imagine it, some images and scenarios may be from bits and pieces you have learned about them along the way. Some may be from logic or intuition. As you tune in to each channel, you see a movie on the screen as if you can see it through their eyes. Suddenly, sound and volume from their internal world become more vivid. You reach for the dial on the panel in front of you, as you maintain control over the level of the volume and the intensity of the picture.

You begin to see how they arrived at their conclusion. Perhaps it was a past hurt, a past trauma, or an event from which they are now triggered. Bring the scene in closer and turn up the volume to a level that you are able to tolerate while still remaining fully encapsulated and insulated by the protective blanket that continues to embrace you.

Wrapped up in the soothing blanket of protection, sit with this scene as a neutral observer of plausible scenes. You see their scenes and begin to hear sounds that they may have experienced. These could be merely customs or daily routines with people who taught them to think the way that they do. Allow yourself to adjust the volume and clarity enough for you to tune in to what it may be like—for just a moment—to be that individual person.

You may hear noise as you see some of the things that plausibly happened to them—possibly some painful events. Allow those scenes to unfold as a movie replaying possible experiences from their past. As you tilt your head to one side or the other, you begin to see how they may have arrived at their position through twists and turns of unfortunate life events. Notice their pain that looms as a tall mountain within their soul. The height and strength of their pain is parallel to the height of their emotional intensity as well as their motivation to remain entrenched in that belief.

Sometimes there are biochemical or neurological processes that drive their thoughts, perceptions, and emotions. It is not necessary to know which came first: the painful event or the biochemical processes that may influence their situation. Just observe . . .

Notice a tidal wave of emotions within them, possibly a roaring tsunami of fear, passion, or perhaps panic that possibly overtakes and overwhelms all logic. You can almost feel tossed to and fro in their tumultuous frenzy. Yet you remain buffered and wrapped up—so secure and sheltered that you remain safe and untouched by the dynamics inside them that you see.

Slowly, you begin to see a plausible pathway of their train of thought, how they interpret the same situations so differently from the way that you do. In some upside-down or convoluted way, you begin to see why and what makes sense to them, while your own beliefs remain shielded, unfettered, untouched, and untainted by them. You see their context, their journey, an insight into their perception. . . or *MIS*-perception.

Take as long as you need to understand . . .

When ready, you can pause the movie, the video clip, turn down the noise, and prepare to leave their internal world. You begin to move back into your original comfortable and familiar place in which you began.

As you push "Pause" on the panel in front of you, the whole scene stops and begins to fade. It becomes smaller and smaller as you move farther and farther away from the person. You are able to leave behind all the intensity, experiences, sounds, smells, and scenes that you have observed. You teleport gently upward again while continually wrapped and embraced in the protection of quietness. As you return to your starting point of safety and distance from them, you begin to reconnect with pleasant aromas, visuals, and soothing sounds. Notice a wonderful, fragrant scent that may have originated from an earlier memory of safety and comfort. Reconnect with a place and time in which you were completely safe. Tune in now to all the soothing elements of those pleasant memories.

Moving back to your original place, you begin to feel a gentle cleansing rain washing down on you, shedding any residual energy from this experience and leaving the person's energy completely behind as you return to your place. Feel this cleansing flow wash over you, as you feel lighter, freer. As you cross back over the boundary you constructed earlier, seeing it still fully intact, you begin to feel a gentle warmth of sunlight shining and caressing you from above. Feel this gentle warmth as you now are crossing back over into your original side. Warm, relieved, and free, you land gently back in the place where you started. You are safe, warm, and free—with new awareness and deep wisdom.

Contemplation Nine: Getting Rid of Shame

―――――― ⚭ ――――――

"The Spirit of the Sovereign Lord is on me,
because the Lord has anointed me
to proclaim good news to the poor.
He has sent me to bind up the brokenhearted,
to proclaim freedom for the captives
and release from darkness for the prisoners,
to proclaim the year of the Lord's favor
and the day of vengeance of our God,
to comfort all who mourn,
and provide for those who grieve in Zion—
to bestow on them a crown of beauty
instead of ashes,
the oil of joy
instead of mourning,
and a garment of praise
instead of a spirit of despair.

They will be called oaks of righteousness,
a planting of the Lord
for the display of his splendor."

Isaiah 61:1-3 (NIV)

Why so sad, my child? Why are you downcast, my precious one? What happened to you is NOT you. Come, let's wash it away completely.

As you look up, you suddenly notice that you are in a beautiful garden with fragrant fresh flowers and beautiful green trees. You see majestic mountains on the horizon. The grass is so soft that you can walk barefoot, so you do. As you walk, with each step, your feet are cushioned and cradled with the soft, rich green grass, and you feel coolness and tenderness supporting you with each step.

You begin to notice a beautiful, rich, warm light shining upon your face from above as it gently caresses your cheeks. There is a breeze that carries a soothing, soft sound with a blend of music like nothing you have ever encountered. It is soft and soothing, yet vibrant and renewing. Allow yourself to breathe in its calming fragrance. All at once, you look above and see that the warm light reaches gently out to you as if to guide you. Notice its soothing aroma and beautiful colors. As it gently reaches around you, you are shown a magnificent waterfall in the distance. You approach it.

Now the sound of the breeze melts into a beautiful rhythmic harmony of this majestic water that flows from high above. See its clear and glistening qualities. Reach out your hand and feel its purifying effects as its mist gently moistens the tips of your fingers. As you allow yourself to become acclimated, you may want to cup your hands and allow the cool, gentle water flow to fill your palms. Take as long as you need. As the water flows, you look up and realize that it is flowing directly from Heaven.

Gradually, you reach your arm into its stream and notice that every part of your body that touches it becomes purified, cleansed, renewed—just as pure as the day you were conceived from Heaven. When ready, allow yourself to step completely beneath this flow of cleansing wholeness. As it washes you physically from the top of your head to the tip of your toes, it also cleanses your soul. You begin to feel yourself being completely purified, cleansed, refreshed, and healed. In this flow from above, you experience a sense of profound safety and newness, as all the past is washed away. You realize that no human being on Earth ever has any power to taint you. There is no trace of anything that has happened to you—all is washed away completely. You see all elements of the past as they are being thoroughly removed from you. They are descending way downstream, further and further away from you. You can see now that there is no trace of anything from the past as it is rapidly being removed and washed away . . . to never return.

Purity and innocence now pour into you. You become clean from your head to your toes and completely pure inside. Notice the tingling vibrant feeling on your skin and throughout your soul. Remain here as long as you need.

As you stand in this cleansing flow, you realize that no one—absolutely no one—has the power to taint you in any way. No one has ever had that power and no one can ever in the future. Your innocence is solid and secure. You are just as clean and innocent as the day you were born. The false images of shame and guilt wash away like a torrential river . . . out and away forever.

Remain in this soothing flow of clear healing for as long as you need and reconnect with it as often as you need.

Contemplation Ten:
How Can I Go On Without You?

Widowhood

———— ◇◇ ————

"No one has power over the spirit to retain the spirit,
And no one has power in the day of death. . . "

Ecclesiastes 8:8 (NKJV)

How can I bear another night without you by my side? The night and even the day get so lonely. I cry a river of tears, and it seems like it will never end.

When—HOW—will this pain ever go away?

I took care of you, but did I do enough? I loved you, but was it enough? I stood by your side, but never perfectly. This is so hard . . . . I wish I could've . . . . should've . . . . would've . . . .

Why did you leave me? Why did you let this happen?? Why couldn't I have stopped it? I had dreams for us. We were supposed to grow old together, visit grandbabies, travel together. It is just NOT fair!

How long will this ache in my heart remain? I can't envision life without you there with me. I don't believe I can do this alone. Why did you go on before me, and I am here without you . . . alone?

Why. . . . .?

Standing there in the midst of a garden, you begin to sense the aroma of your favorite scents in nature. If you find it comforting, tune in also perhaps to the aroma of your loved one's favorite scents as well or maybe their cologne. Notice a wealth of warmth around you as you look up and begin to see God's loving hands reaching gently toward you.

You almost lift up your voice in protest to raise up the barrage of questions that you have been holding so tightly inside that your throat feels like a lump that won't dislodge. All at once you begin to see an opening in the distance on the horizon.

What is this? As you move closer to a clearing set prominently on the horizon, you begin to see an image emerge. As you move still closer, it becomes larger and its details become more transparent.

Now as you breathe in the soothing, fragrant scent of this place, mingled with the light flowing from the horizon, you notice that it brings a mixture of calmness and strength to your soul. The opening widens and illuminates as God allows you a peek into your loved one's experience. As you recall in John 3:16 that God so loved the (whole) world that he gave his Son to save each of us, His children, you are able to see your loved one bathed in God's mercy and forgiveness. You are able to see your loved one safe and sound in the arms of God.

You ask—

Why did this happen?

A video emerges on the horizon and begins to play. As you see glimpses of images, perhaps it shows you future experiences that your loved one may have been spared. It also begins to show you their lifetime of so many achievements that were overlooked by the world. The time they helped someone in secret or the time when they bit their tongue and resisted a challenging impulse. You see innumerable times of behavior and sacrifices of which no one had been aware. In this video, you hear a loud, thunderous applause in Heaven for kindness they showed throughout their entire life while receiving little or no recognition here on Earth. They have graduated from a life filled with challenges. Now they are being rewarded with rest, peace, eternal love, hope, and safety.

You look closer and begin to see each area in which they had formerly suffered physical pain while on the Earth. Now you can see them being completely healed and made new. A soothing balm wraps around their soul and heals them, ameliorating every part of their heart that had been broken in life's rough experiences. In this moment, you are given a close-up, firsthand view of their soul being completely healed, completely renewed. They are now free from every disease, even if hidden, both physically and mentally—completely healed and made new. They are now innocent, cleansed, and new—just as the day they were born.

They are wrapped up in the perfect soothing, loving arms of God.

You ask—

How can I do this alone?

As the warmth above wraps around you, you begin to hear tender words. *"My child, you are not alone. Your rewards await you as well, but not just yet - I know the plans that I have for you, as I have said in Jeremiah 29:11 and I will be with you helping you do so many things ahead. You still have a purpose here on this earth, and as I said in John 14:12-17, you will be able to do more than you think you can. I am with you. Remember what I promised in Hebrews 13:5, that I will never leave you nor forsake you. I am here with you, and you are not alone."*

All at once, that same warm light begins to strengthen like a protection and wrap you up in a safe cocoon. You also notice that you are still closely connected to your soul mate even while they exist just next door in eternity, and you exist here on Earth. Your connection to them remains and will never end. Feel the strength of this connection to that loved one now as you remember how much they loved you and you them. While you remain here on Earth, still connected to your loved one in spirit—just as if they are only in the next room—you also are being wrapped up in the strong arms of God. Everywhere you go, you are still safe, still strong, and covered—protected by the hand of God.

You are not alone. And you do

not have to do this alone.

Contemplation Eleven: Breaking Free From Emotional Ties

———— ∞ ————

"Brothers and sisters, I do not consider myself yet to have taken hold of it.

But one thing I do: Forgetting what is behind and straining toward what is ahead."

Philippians 3:13 (NIV)

Feeling it slip away, slip right through your fingers. Day by day you can feel them slipping away.

The affection? The respect? The closeness that once was in your relationship? Or perhaps it is their very life and existence in yours?

How do you let go? This was so special and precious. This has been important for such a very long time. *Seriously??* Let go of the person. The dream.

How?

You look at what lies behind, and right now that may be all that you see. The memories. The fun. The past.

The courage to look at what is in front of you may seem filled with mystery, uncertainty, perhaps fear, and . . . HOPE.

As you sit in a large theater, you see three large blank movie screens. Embrace the privacy that you have here in this room. In the imagery of your mind, you may want to invite supportive loved ones to be near you. Even some who have gone on before can have a place of support here. You also may have a favorite pet, or you can imagine a friend by your side. You can also imagine yourself surrounded by Angels.

Allow yourself to feel the presence of these supportive ones near you. You may feel them sitting right beside you or perhaps positioned in various places in this theater room. Notice their scent. Breathe in the pleasant aroma of their scent. Perhaps you can feel their presence through gentle touch. Notice anything and everything around you, giving it a soothing texture—the seat where you sit, perhaps the fur of your pet nestled closely beside you.

Now, while anchored in safety with supportive ones, allow your attention to turn to one of the three movie screens.

Screen 1: The first screen addresses the loss of a job, situation, or opportunity, or alternatively, the loss of a friend, partner, or companion due to their decision to leave the relationship.

Screen 2: The second screen addresses the loss of a loved one through death or transitioning into the afterlife.

Screen 3: The third movie screen represents a glimpse into the future that is there for you. This is a screen of HOPE.

Before you turn your attention to Screen 3, it is important to view Screen 1 or 2. You can view both if you need to do so.

Allow yourself to choose one of the screens below:

Screen 1

On this screen, you begin to hear soft music playing. You notice that the tune is very sad. As the tune plays, images begin to emerge on the screen about losses, but these are not your losses. To your surprise, you begin to see the greater loss that the job, opportunity, or person is losing by leaving you. Allow yourself to notice all the features and/or blessings that you have, whether few or many, with that person or situation. They will no longer have your friendship, your generosity, or whatever it is that you provided for them. Perhaps you laughed at their jokes or even put up with more than others would have.

While it is necessary for you to grieve your loss of that person or opportunity, you are now able to recognize what a loss this is to them as well. Take all the time you need to view this screen and revisit it as often as you need to do so.

Screen 2

As you turn to Screen 2, allow yourself to see the loved one. It may be a person or a beloved pet. Allow yourself to visualize an image of them as if they are merely going into the next room. This is a room where they will no longer suffer. If they suffered from a long illness or a brief injury, all that pain vanishes instantly when they move through the door into that room. You begin to realize that this room also serves another purpose. As you see them there, an acute awareness arises, showing you other traumas from which they were completely spared. Now, they are resting peacefully, experiencing bliss in the arms of their creator, who holds them.

There is a stream of light that flows from them to you even as they pass through that door. This light represents your connection, your mutual love for each other that remains attached forever. Notice how your connection to them remains steady, strong, and solid. Feel the strength of this enduring connection as they are just on the other side. Their love for you remains completely intact and continues for eternity.

Screen 3

Now, turn to the third screen. This is a screen to help you begin to envision a future beyond that person, loving pet, or opportunity. At first, it may seem very difficult to see any future at all without that person or situation you cherished so dearly in your life. It is natural to find it challenging to imagine your life without what was before.

As you look up at this third screen, it may seem dark or cloudy at first. Allow yourself to notice a light that begins to shine down from Heaven onto the screen. As the light shines onto that screen, allow the image of your future to emerge. This may be a very small picture, as you gently give yourself time to adjust.

Allow a very small picture of yourself to emerge on the screen. As you see yourself without that person or situation, you can begin to realize that you are not alone. The light from Heaven begins to fill in the space that is missing from their absence and the change in your life. If you have lost a loved one, you can glance at Screen 2, where you can see that your connection to them still remains, while they have moved into that next room of comfort and no pain. You can ask what this loved one would now wish for you in your life and in your future.

As you look back again at Screen 3, which represents your new hope, you also can begin to see, hear, and imagine an opportunity for which you may have set aside in your life. You may have totally forgotten an activity that you may have been too busy to even think about or consider before. Now that there is a little more space and time in your life, begin to allow yourself to see right there on the screen the small budding of an opportunity.

As you glance back at Screen 2, you may see a nod of blessing from that loved one for you to begin to consider that opportunity now.

You may glance back to Screen 1 and see how the loss of that job or career may be turning into a blessing in disguise.

Allow yourself to make the image of new possibilities on Screen 3 become larger, more vibrant, and gradually increase in volume until it is clearer to you than ever before. There may be a distinct aroma associated with this new possibility. Take it in. Take as much time as you need with this image on Screen 3. Notice the new colors, sounds, aromas, and textures of the new reality that is forming right before your eyes.

Revisit Screen 3 as often as you can, each time allowing its sound, visual image, and aroma to increase. Give yourself patience. Letting go requires a grieving period. Give yourself permission to take all the time you need to grieve while you begin acclimating to your new vision in this process. Be gentle with yourself in your pace of letting go. With each time you revisit Screen 3, you may begin to notice a feeling of anticipation, exhilaration, or excitement begin to gradually replace the grief as you consider your possible encounter with this new adventure.

Each new chapter in your life brings for you an opportunity to discover your new purpose. You can create a new adventure. Allow yourself time to create and expand your new dream.

Contemplation Twelve: Forgiveness: How to Forgive

Part I
How to Forgive Others

"For now we see only a reflection as in a mirror; then we shall see face to face. Now I know in part; then I shall know fully, even as I am fully known."

1 Corinthians 13:12 (NIV)

"The Lord is close to the brokenhearted and saves those who are crushed in spirit."

Psalm 34:18 (NIV)

I magine that you are in a very safe, secure place. Surround yourself with everything that you need for support. You may picture Angels, God, Jesus, your loving supportive relatives, dear and favorite pets— anyone and everything that you need. These will be your buffer and distance from the person with whom it may have been difficult to forgive and move beyond.

Now, at a safe distance, use your imagination to set out in front of you the person who hurt you. Set them out as far away as you need for them to be. Envision them at a distance far enough for your comfort. Notice how far away they are and how buffered you are, surrounded by your loved ones and spiritual resources of strength. Now, include in this imagery any additional boundaries that you need. This could be a wall or you can imagine that you are in a sphere surrounded by God and Angels. Take all the time you need to set this up in such a way that you feel completely safe.

As you look out upon that person who hurt you, allow yourself to apply a multidimensional perspective about them, right there as you view them from a safe distance. This person is going to remain silent and still. They are not in a position to speak or say anything at all. In this imagery, they are frozen in time.

Knowing what we know about human development, people become stunted at the age in which they experienced a deficit. This deficit can be in the form of a trauma or simply a lack of instruction. Allow yourself, in the safety of your distance from them, to observe them with neutral eyes for a moment. In this imagery, we do not have to know anything specifically; all we need to know is that what people do to you and me is about them more than it is about you or me. What might have been their trauma or lack of instruction? Allow yourself to ponder the following questions for just a moment without needing to know exact details or verification. What might have happened to them? Was there possibly trauma? Emotional, physical, or even sexual abuse? As a child, were they unable to seek comfort or trust in another human being? Were they bereft of healthy mentoring, misled by dysfunctional influences, or perhaps deprived of positive role models? Were they experiencing a possible biochemical imbalance in their body or brain?

You can ask God, Jesus, the Holy Spirit, or your intuitive wisdom to help you ponder what might be plausible. This awareness is only through imagery and is only for you at this moment. The information that emerges about this person is what may be logical, conceivable, or probable. There is no need to confirm its veracity, nor to confront the person with this information. This perception to imagine and consider is designed for You and you alone and to show you an awareness that can launch you into freedom, a Higher Order Perspective Existence (H.O.P.E.).[1]

Allow yourself to imagine what may have stunted their emotional sensitivity or behavior for the purpose of bringing to your mind an ability to rise above and overcome. This process neither makes excuses for them nor lets them off the hook. This image is also not for the purpose of having you feel sorry for them, as everyone has a free choice. This is only for *YOUR* emotional freedom.

Now, asking God to show you the earliest age that this deficit may have gotten started for them, you look at the image of the person, and they begin to shrink down to that earliest age. Remaining safe behind all your protection, what do you see? What age do you see in them? Do you see them suddenly shrinking down to a teenager? A toddler? Allow yourself to see their *earliest age* in which they first

---

[1] Dr. Joan Weathersbee Ellason. *Finally…….The How to of Forgiveness, A Three-Tier Approach to Dry Your Tears,* Oasis Workshops, 2020.

became deprived of what was supposed to be taught to them or poured into their soul. Now, as you look with more clarity, you may see them at the age of four or five, or even as an infant in the crib.

Take a moment and focus on this new, smaller image of that person as you are at a safe distance, and they are just sitting still and quiet, just as a frozen image in front of you. Notice this image now before you. Notice perhaps impoverishment or emptiness as it becomes apparent that some important emotional and spiritual nurturance may not have been deposited into them. Do they appear pale or thin? Perhaps crouched down or weakened? See them in their weakened state. As with a laser-like view, you are able to see a glimpse into their soul for just a moment.

Allow yourself to now see, right beside them, a huge vending machine. This vending machine is supposed to be there for your replenishment, if you are thirsty or hungry or need a resource of some sort. The front of the glass cover is completely clear so that you can see inside its contents. However, in this vending machine, as you look behind the clear glass, you see that it is *completely empty.* Every socket where a refreshment is supposed to be available is completely absent. You could put dollar after dollar in all day long and retrieve *absolutely nothing!* It is *just not in there!*

Now look back at the image of the person, who is now still in child form, empty and gaunt. Everything you needed from them, likely, was and is just not there—just like the machine. When you were interacting with them in a relationship and it hurt that they did not produce the much dearly needed response, was it *this* person you see who was really at the wheel? This wounded soul inside an adult image may have just simply not had what you were needing, no matter how hard they tried. Was this perhaps the one who you were really encountering when on the outside you believed you were interacting with a grown adult, parent, mature spouse, partner, or friend? Notice that wounded inner child who may have hidden inside a fully grown adult body, trying to be your parent all along, but completely inept, depleted, vacant of what was needed to fulfill that role. Like a vending machine completely empty of anything that you wanted, it may just not have been in there—not in them.

As you observe what is real about this image, whether we know for certain what might have actually stunted their soul, three things are true:

- What you needed was just not in there.

- You now begin to realize that it was not your fault that they could not and did not give you what you needed.

- As you allow yourself to be released from false blame, you also begin to realize that it is God's job and not yours to fix *them*.

You may have been trying to get them to heal, change, and treat you the way you needed to, to no avail, and you realize that not only is it not your fault, but God is the ultimate healer, and they are the only ones who can make those choices. As you see them in this light, you also become aware that it is their responsibility to decide whether to change, grow, or remain wounded—*not yours.* Everyone is given free choice, and now as you look at them, you are able to see them with the awareness that it is not your job to fix them. This is between them and their Creator. At this point, the effort you may have been exercising to get them to change, repent, and see the gravity of what they have done can be handed back to them. Allow yourself to hand over any and all false responsibility you may have carried for them—it is theirs—not yours. You can choose to free your energy back up—take all your energy back to channel into your God-given purpose instead.

When you are ready, proceed to do this. As you begin to hand all that responsibility, effort, and time spent back to them, you begin to feel fatigue leave your body. See all your fatigue and burden move over to them. Continue until you have freed yourself of all its weight, so that you can give this task back to them and release it to God.

As you take one last look at this image, allow yourself to literally hand them up to God and move them totally off your plate. This job is higher than the human skill set. You begin to see them float all the way up to the upper corner of your periphery, and they move slowly up into the hand of God. For this is their place of repair. Allow them to move into the hands of God until they are completely out of your sight and off your plate.

Everything that you had needed from that person is legitimate and still valid. The next thing you see will be a new resource for those needs.

As you turn away from where their image had been, you begin to notice a beautiful, strong, sturdy staircase that leads all the way up to Heaven. Allow yourself to take hold of the handrail and notice that it has a loving warmth and soothing feel to it. Allow yourself to go step by step all the way up to the place where your needs are valued and you are safe.

As you reach the top and begin to look out onto a beautiful field of clouds, you notice a gentle, loving breeze flowing through your hair and a warm ray of sunshine gently caressing your face. Up here you can leave any pain of Earth behind. Any grieving can be set aside for a later time as you come up to this place to be replenished.

Perhaps you plop down on a field of soft white fluffy clouds, or perhaps rest under a tree in this place. Feel the beautiful warm sun on your cheeks and breathe in an aroma of peace and security that is nothing like you have ever experienced before. This is a place of retreat.

And you realize that your needs are still legitimate. Everything that you needed from someone who was not able to give to you can be received from the very one who created you and loves you the most. Allow yourself to notice that all at once, you see the Creator of the Universe, God, Jesus, the Holy Spirit, gazing into your eyes with a love that surpasses anything that you have ever experienced on Earth—ever. You begin to feel this Divine Love flow as a river from deep into your heart and into your soul. It fills, soothes, and replenishes all areas that had been formerly drained, fatigued, or burdened. Connect with the physical sense of this river of love flowing and filling you with renewed energy, love, hope, and purpose. You begin to become refreshed and restored.

Allow yourself to receive unconditional love in this place. You may hand over to your Creator anything that has been painful, and in exchange, you are given a wealth of healing from the one who knows you and loves you more than anyone has ever been able to.

As you look up into the eyes of the Creator, allow yourself to hear what you have needed that the broken human could not give to you. Tune in as you begin to hear God's loving words now spoken to you. You may begin to feel a tangible sense of being gently wrapped in the arms of God, Jesus, your Creator, as you hear long-needed replenishment.

Perhaps you hear, "I am proud of you." " I have created you for a purpose, and you are going to be able to accomplish it. I will help you succeed." "I love you more than you know." "You are the apple of my eye." "You are enough." "You are precious in my sight." "I forgive you." "You are clean and pure in my sight." "You do not have to bear anything alone." "I am with you." "I will never leave you." "You are my precious child."

Take as long as you need in this place.

Rest here as you become completely filled with everything that you need. When you are ready, bring all this love and truth back with you to the very place where you sit. Keep all these messages in your heart and return here as often as you need to do so.

Forgiveness: How to Forgive

Part II
How to Forgive Yourself

*"....as far as the east is from the west,
so far has he removed our transgressions from us."*

Psalm 103:12 (NIV)

*"The steadfast love of the Lord never ceases,
his mercies never come to an end;
they are new every morning;
great is your faithfulness."*

Lamentations 3:22–23 (NRSVue)

"The Lord appeared to us in the past, saying:

'I have loved you with an everlasting love;
I have drawn you with unfailing kindness.'"

Jeremiah 31:3 (NIV)

This is a journey into the mercies of God. As you see yourself in this   process, there will be no judgment, no shame, no condemnation. In this imagery, there will only be simple, neutral observation to allow yourself to see beyond what you may have seen before.

Take a moment to create a buffer of strength, emotional safety, and protection around yourself. Feel free to bring in support. Do you wish to include angels? Jesus? Supportive loved ones? Take all the time you need to wrap yourself in love, safety, and mercy as you embark on this journey.

Develop this blanket of safety with fullness like a cocoon. Give it a texture. Is it a soft blanket of warmth? Is it a solid armor of strength? Is it thick? Is it illuminated with brilliance? Make it be whatever you need it to be. Give it a soothing aroma, a warm and cozy feel, and a comforting color. Begin to feel yourself wrapped in this protective boundary that will allow this experience to be emotionally gentle for you.

When you become ready, you can float above your lifespan at a distance. You can remain at this distance throughout the whole time if you wish. You are in charge of your level of closeness or detachment during this exercise, and the focus will only be viewed as a still, freeze-frame image—emotionally removed.

Now, while wrapped up in your cocoon of protection, go back to a moment of regret. See the event in freeze-frame form as a neutral photo of that moment, while viewed from above. You may notice a shaded veil or gentle fog that protects you from seeing unnecessary detail. The main focus in the image is you and what you may have overlooked about yourself in that moment.

Take a moment to acknowledge that this is a picture of a human being on a journey in an imperfect world. At the moment of this regret, you begin to notice a light shining from the Heavens, illuminating new information that you may not have dialed into your awareness. Beneath that action, what were you feeling at that very moment? Were you scared? Were you depleted? Were you feeling helpless? Were you overwhelmed? Were you too young? Did you need more knowledge about how to handle that situation at the time?

What was missing that you needed? Rest? Knowledge? Information? Tools? Help to carry part of the load you were trying to handle on your own? There is no blame here. These are not excuses. These are logical facts. These are no more excuses than a machine that did or did not do what was expected because it was not serviced or a car being blamed when it is running low on oil, gas, or electrical charge. You cannot blame yourself for what was missing from your arsenal at that time.

Take time to observe what was missing and was not your fault. Notice that life is a journey of learning. Remember when you might have tried to learn how to ride a bike or perhaps some other skill? Recall the process of trial and error in that task. Notice the permission for mistakes in that process. Bring that awareness and permission back into the scene of your moment of regret.

Observe your intention beneath the action. Again, the light from Heaven shines down gently upon that image of You in that situation. Now you are able to see your intentions. Allow yourself to see through the situation and into the heart of what you were meaning to accomplish in that moment. Were you trying to get them to leave you alone, to stop pressuring you? Were you trying to protect someone? Allow God to show you the tenderness of your heart beneath the event. God sees you through the eyes of mercy.

As the light continues to illuminate this image of you, you may notice an even younger you who had been only operating from what was not given to them in the past.

With a safe distance and only neutral observation, trace this moment back to the earliest time that you had done something like this or seen someone do something like this before. Allow yourself to see this earliest moment also at a great distance and as if through a fog. Continue to stay safely protected and buffered, wrapped up in protection. We are _not_ going to relive anything that has happened before, for it is not necessary. Just simply notice that earliest time and freeze the frame or picture as well.

Within the freeze-frame still image that you can only see through a fog, notice the emotions that were influencing that younger child, which was you. At that very first moment, were you scared? Were you pressured? Did you believe that you had no options?

Take your time, as you only need to notice from a distance, features that you may not have been able to see before. Now, from this objective distance, you also begin to see how young, how small, and perhaps how unprepared you were at that time.

Expand the scene for a moment to allow yourself to notice what was missing that you needed. Were others influencing you wrongly? Were you pressured? Scared? Trapped? Were people you needed to be there to help or guide you absent from you? Were you uninformed or misled? Were you in the position of fending for yourself far too early in your life?

Who nurtured you in this scene? Who taught you the right things to do in this moment? Who rescued you?

Would you like to get rid of all that sadness and regret? Would you like to pour all of it out and take up your energy now for good and fruitfulness in your life?

The Heavens open wider above now with a brilliant light. Allow yourself to see God, Jesus, your Creator, reaching out His arms with His mighty and immense hands cupped and open in front of you. Now, allow yourself to pour them all out—all those regrets—into His hands. It is time to make room for your new positive energy, hope, and love to fill that space that was so long occupied by a debt that was already paid off.

Visualize all your mistakes being poured into God's hands. As you see this, something amazing happens. Every single mistake and regret begins to melt. As it all melts, what emerges before your eyes is an abundant overflow of mercy. See His mercy as it fills the space where you are. Notice its gentleness. Notice that it is a continual flow.

What was once overwhelming becomes overflowing. What was once draining becomes fulfilling. What was once depleting becomes renewing. Take all the time you need in this new flow of mercy and forgiveness. Allow it to fill up your heart.

After you have remained in this place for as long as you need, there is yet one more task to fulfill. Going back to the image of you—that child who was perhaps overwhelmed or misguided. With your heart now filled with God's mercy, look closely at that scene. In the image, notice the you that was. Even while still at a distance, notice what you may see now that you may not have seen before. You may see a glimpse of tender, innocent eyes, a heart of one perhaps feeling defenseless and not knowing what to do.

Take all that mercy you received from God and

now become the nurturing parent to yourself that you needed back then. Allow yourself to pour mercy into your own heart, as God wants all of us—His children—to be filled with His mercy and love.

While the scene is still set at freeze-frame, and depending on your comfort zone of distance versus connection, you may want to walk into that scene and pick up that child . . . YOU. . . the child who has been waiting for someone to come and nurture them to help them grow.

Here you may be able to tell this child—YOU—
what you have needed.

If you are ready, you can kneel down, eye-to-eye, face-to-face, and say, "I am going to learn how to take care of you now. I am going to learn how to teach you constructively about better options and how to have a better life." Allow yourself to tell you, "I love you." Or "I am learning how to love." And "This was not your fault. I forgive you."

You get to be the healthy parent now.

You may also choose to take that child—You—up in your arms and bring them close to your heart. Tell them that they did that because they were scared/hurt/did not know better/needed protection/_____ fill in the words that needed to be said but were not said at that time.

Allow yourself to bring that child—You—back to a safe place in the here and now. You can tell them, "I will learn to take care of you now. I see your innocence and that you were acting out of fear, a lack of guidance, or limited options . . ."

Take as much time as you need to bring You back—out of the past and into a new future with your wisdom, guidance, mercy, and a new start.

Today you get to make a new beginning. You get to rewrite this story about you.

". . . how often I have longed to gather your children together, as a hen gathers her chicks under her wings . . . "

Luke 13:34 (NIV)

MISTAKES can become cleansed and transformed into

MERCY . . . .

MISTAKES

---❦---

MERCIES

    IMMACULATELY

      SECURED

        TO

          ACHIEVE

            KNOWLEDGE

              ETHICS &

                SUCCESS

Into...MERCY

MIRACULOUS

EMANCIPATION

REDEMPTION

COMPASSION for

YOU

Forgiveness: How to Forgive

—————— ❦ ——————

Part III
Permission to Forgive Yourself

"....as far as the east is from the west,
so far has he removed our transgressions from us.
"

Psalm 103:12 (NIV)

You are suddenly transported back in time to 2,000 years ago. You look down to find your scantily clothed feet covered in dust with tattered sandals. The road is long.

Your attention is captured by a massive commotion up ahead. You hear the noise of cries and wails, screams and calamity. What is going on? You must see what this is. So, you make your way closer until you reach the crowd. Now, much closer, the noise reverberates in your ears like nothing you have ever heard before. It is almost overwhelming.

Nevertheless, you press your way through that crowd, elbow to elbow, ignoring the grungy smell of sweat and stench from the people. You've got to see what this is! Suddenly you notice a unique scent of dogwood, and you see a tall, massive structure towering above your head. It appears as if someone is struggling beneath its weight. Now, as you get even closer, you see tall soldiers surrounding something or . . . someone? Who is this?

The crowd now almost engulfs you, tightly squeezing you within. You ignore it as you make your way through the soldiers, the noise, and the chaos. You finally break through and see what is at the center of this horrific commotion.

There in the midst, you see the back of someone covered with dirt, bruises, and lacerations who is leaning forward and struggling beneath the weight of the tall wooden structure. Who *is* this person, and what has he done to deserve any of this?

You are within arm's reach of him now. As you stretch out your hand and touch his moist shoulder, you feel his sweat and blood now on your fingertips. All at once, he stops and spins around, face-to-face and eye-to-eye with you. So close that you feel his breath on your face. A pure light shines from Jesus' kind, loving eyes that soothes your heart and soul like nothing you have ever encountered before here on this Earth. Now, in a soft voice so clear, Jesus says directly to you, "I forgive you this much. I FORGIVE YOU *THIS* MUCH!*"

He goes on to say to you tenderly, "Please let go of all that anger toward yourself. You are innocent in my eyes. Can you fathom how precious you are to me? I am paying dearly for you, paying a price to cover all your mistakes and regrets, so that you can live the fruitful life that I have planned for you. I can handle what you cannot bear. Will you allow me to save you from the broken pieces of your life? Hand them all over to me now, all your regrets and past mistakes . . . all your fears. I can take them all and make them into an amazing new beginning."

"I love you with a love that goes beyond anything

that you have ever known....

I love you, eternally."